The DNA Alphabet

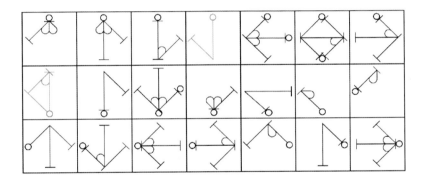

VH Frater BT

Dedicated to Isaac Newton

With one foot in the occult
tradition of spiritual alchemy,
the other grounded in pure reason,
so dedicated was he to
the pursuit of hidden knowledge
that he became known as
the father of modern science.

CONTENTS

The Word becomes flesh,
and dwells amongst us.

I. INTRODUCTION

Once upon a time, in 1996, I was at once a High School Junior and a Practicus in a Golden Dawn style initiatory Order which I now lovingly refer to as "The Procrustean Order of the Limited Value Intl.™" (or "POLVI").

On Wednesday nights and weekends, I was beginning to work with sigil-magic, and on weekdays, for 43 minutes a day, I was learning introductory molecular biology.

In my science textbook was an overview of how the permutations of **the four nucleic acids** of the **messenger RNA** (mRNA) were "read" by the **ribosomes**, and how each group of three of these four nucleic acids, the groups of three being called **codons**, would translate into one of the **20 amino acids** to be arranged into various kinds of **proteins**, such as peptides and enzymes.

My mind, at the time, was swimming in and saturated by the 22 Hebrew Letters with their Astrological and Tarot correspondences, as well as The Four Worlds of the Kabbalah signified by the Divine Name YHVH (יהוה) and the corresponding Four Elements, etc.

So, rather than paying attention to what the teacher was saying, I began drawing these little symbols in the margins of my textbook beside the codon table. These same symbols are the subject of the book you are now reading.

What it isn't

This book is not intended as a substitute for a course in molecular biology or genetics, and certainly not a substitute for medicine or well-informed nutrition. It may serve, however, as an introduction to some of these concepts for those who are not already familiar with them.

What it is

The DNA Alphabet presented here is a concise distillation of what can be considered The Natural Language. It is The Language of Life itself: Human beings, viruses, cacti, dinosaurs, all plants, mushrooms, and insects share a common language, the language in which they themselves are written.

In this book, you'll learn the 20 letters of The DNA Alphabet, The Natural Language. You'll learn to write these letters in the same way that they are written by the DNA. Then, you'll begin to learn some basic words, in form of peptides, which we already interact with in every moment of every day.

By reducing the complex processes to simple shapes and movements, our minds can begin to grasp, intuit, and to become familiar with the organic processes.

The DNA Alphabet as presented here can be as useful to a beginner as it can be to one with a master's degree in molecular biology. Rather than relying on Monsanto and Crispr to understand the language of ourselves for us, we can begin to speak and eventually become fluent in The Language of Life.

How you can use it

There are at least three ways to approach this book:

1. Learning these letters can help you memorize the codons, the permutations which produce the amino acids.

2. The simple distillation can be an object of contemplation, allowing for a deeper understanding of and relationship with Nature.

3. The Letters and Words can be traced in the air, or upon a talisman, to signal our DNA by way of the subconscious mind to produce more or less of a particular amino acid, peptide, or enzyme.

Further, the Alphabet as presented in this book can serve as a starting point for you to develop your own way to better understand, memorize, and work with DNA.

First, we'll read about the Letters, and how the symbols encapsulate the way the DNA stores, awakens, and reawakens the many and various activities of the body and brain. Then, I'll go into a bit more mercurial depth as to the process by which I derived these Letters. Finally, we'll learn some of the basic Words, the peptides by which we govern our states of mind and body.

II. THE LETTERS

When a magician draws a simple sigil, they begin with a circle. The circle indicates the beginning point, usually a letter or number on a pre-established key, such as the Rose Cross Lamen or the Planetary Kameas. A line then extends from that circle to the position of the next letter or number. It ends with a small perpendicular line.

For our purposes, the pre-established key is the four nucleic acids arranged in an equal-armed cross formation:

When using the ideas of language in reference to DNA and mRNA, some people refer to the nucleic acids as the "letters." However, in this book the nucleic acids are the points we will use to create the Letters, which are the amino acids. Thus, there are 20 Letters in The DNA Alphabet as presented here, not 4.

The DNA Alphabet

The 20 Letters are given in the book in a kind of DNA-Alphabetical order. This is explained thoroughly later, in the section called "DNA-Alphabetical."

For now, if you would like to skip to a particular amino acid, they are listed here with the page numbers, in conventional alphabetical order using the Latin letters of their names:

Lysine

Popularized in fiction by Jurassic Park, Lysine in real life helps with energy metabolism, protein stability, vision, and many other things.

For Humans, it is one of the **9 essential amino acids**. It is necessary for the spelling of Words (proteins and peptides), but the body cannot produce it on its own, so it must be received in food.

It can be found in meat, including fish, as well as eggs and cheese, especially Parmesan. Vegans can get it from soy, spirulina, and fenugreek seed.

Before you go buy a bunch of supplements, though, consult a doctor or nutrition specialist, as too much Lysine can be unhealthy. Balance is key.

There are 2 mRNA codons which each invoke, or call upon, Lysine:

Adenine-Adenine-Adenine (top-top-top), or Adenine-Adenine-Guanine (top-top-left).

Asparagine

Asparagine is necessary for brain function and development.

It is called non-essential. This just means that it is produced within the Human body, but it is still a good idea to receive some through food. Too much, though, can be unhealthy.

Asparagine is produced from the Letter Aspartate by an enzyme/Word of 561 Letters known as Asparagine Synthetase, whose name is written in the number 7 **chromosome** of the Human DNA.

Either of these 2 mRNA codons will invoke Asparagine:

Adenine-Adenine-Uracil (top-top-bottom), or Adenine-Adenine-Cytosine (top-top-right).

Isoleucine

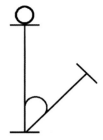

Isoleucine is necessary for growth, Glucose metabolism and transportation, and the immune system.

It is one of the 9 essential amino acids, so it must be received in food. It can be found in meat and fish, as well as soy, and seaweed. Too much Isoleucine can be unhealthy.

Any of these 3 mRNA codons will invoke Isoleucine:

Adenine-Uracil-Adenine (top-bottom-top), Adenine-Uracil-Uracil (top-bottom-bottom), or Adenine-Uracil-Cytosine (top-bottom-right).

Methionine
or START

Methionine is important for the growth of new blood vessels. It the precursor to the Letter Cysteine, as well as that of other amino acids (outside of those in The DNA Alphabet) and compounds. It also helps to maintain hair color.

It is one of the 9 essential amino acids, so it must be received in food. It can be found in meat, fish, eggs, as well as sesame seeds, Brazil nuts, and cereal grains. Too much Methionine can be unhealthy.

There is only 1 mRNA codon which invokes Methionine: Adanine-Uracil-Guanine (top-bottom-left).

This same codon, Adanine-Uracil-Guanine, is also the START command for the mRNA to begin copying any Word from the DNA. It is just before the beginning of every Word in the DNA, and when it is serving as the START command it does not also mean Methionine. If a Word actually needs to start with a Methionine, this Letter will be written twice in a row at the beginning.

Thus, this Letter is either Methionine or START.

Arginine

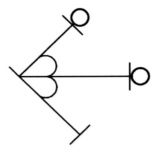

Arginine serves as a healer of wounds, and assists in kidney, immune, and hormone function. It also dilates and relaxes arteries.

It is called conditionally-essential because premature babies are unable to produce Arginine internally. Otherwise, it can be produced inside the body, but it is still a good idea to receive some through food. Too much, though, can be unhealthy.

Any of these 6 mRNA codons will invoke Arginine:

Adenine-Guanine-Adenine (top-left-top), Adenine-Guanine-Guanine (top-left-left), Cytosine-Guanine-Adenine (right-left-top), Cytosine-Guanine-Uracil (right-left-bottom), Cytosine-Guanine-Guanine (right-left-left), or Cytosine-Guanine-Cytosine (right-left-right).

Serine

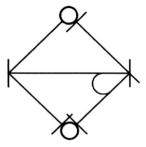

Serine is involved in the creation of purines and pyrimidines like the four nucleic acids, without which there would be no DNA. It is also the precursor to several other amino acids including Glycine and Cysteine, and many other important molecules.

It is non-essential, meaning it is produced within the Human body, but it is still a good idea to receive some through food.

Any of these 6 mRNA codons will invoke Serine:

Adenine-Guanine-Uracil (top-left-bottom), Adenine-Guanine-Cytosine (top-left-right), Uracil-Cytosine-Adenine (bottom-right-top), Uracil-Cytosine-Uracil (bottom-right-bottom), Uracil-Cytosine-Guanine (bottom-right-left), or Uracil-Cytosine-Cytosine (bottom-right-right).

Threonine

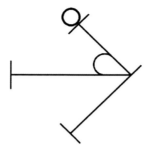

Threonine helps with metabolism, and the production of the immune system's T-cells.

It is one of the 9 essential amino acids, so it must be received in food. It can be found in meat, fish, eggs, milk products, as well as black turtle bean, sesame seeds, green peas, seeds, and nuts. Too much Threonine can be unhealthy.

Any of these 4 codons will invoke Threonine:

Adenine-Cytosine-Adenine (top-right-top), Adenine-Cytosine-Uracil (top-right-bottom), Adenine-Cytosine-Guanine (top-right-left), or Adenine-Cytosine-Cytosine (top-right-right).

STOP

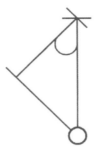

Reminiscent of the old telegraph, instead of a period or a space, there is a sort of Letter whose sole function is to tell the mRNA that a Word is finished.

Any of these 3 codons will signal the mRNA to STOP copying a Word:

Uracil-Adenine-Adenine (bottom-top-top), Uracil-Adenine-Guanine (bottom-top-left), or Uracil-Guanine-Adenine (bottom-left-top)

That said, when encoded by a special tRNA, Uracil-Guanine-Adenine (bottom-left-top) will invoke the 21st Letter, the non-essential amino acid Selenocysteine:

Tyrosine

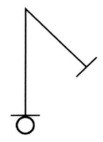

Tyrosine is necessary for photosynthesis to take place. While this is not directly related to internal Human concerns, it is obviously very important, especially to all the multicellular orgasms on the planet. Without Tyrosine, there would be no plant life.

As for more immediate Human concerns, Tyrosine is a precursor to L-DOPA, which is a precursor to the neurotransmitter Dopamine, which is of course very popular.

It is called conditionally-essential since it cannot be produced internally by people with Phenylketonuria. Otherwise, it is produced within the body, but it is still a good idea to receive some through food. Too much, though, can be unhealthy.
.

Either of these 2 mRNA codons will invoke Tyrosine:

Uracil-Adenine-Uracil (bottom-top-bottom), or Uracil-Adenine-Cytosine (bottom top right).

Leucine

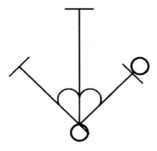

Leucine helps to regulate tissue regeneration and metabolism, and can give energy to skeletal muscles during exercise. It also helps generate Adenosine Triphosphate, which provides energy for intracellular signaling, DNA and RNA synthesis, synaptic signaling, active transport, muscle contraction, and several other important processes.

It is one of the 9 essential amino acids, so it must be received in food. It can be found in meat, fish, eggs, milk products, as well as soy, beans, and other legumes. Too much Leucine can be unhealthy.

Any of these 6 mRNA codons will invoke Leucine:

Uracil-Uracil-Adenine (bottom-bottom-top), Uracil-Uracil-Guanine (bottom-bottom-left), Cytosine-Uracil-Adenine (right-bottom-top), Cytosine-Uracil-Uracil (right-bottom-bottom), Cytosine-Uracil-Guanine (right-bottom-left), or Cytosine-Uracil-Cytosine (right-bottom-right).

Phenylalanine

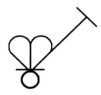

Popularized by the fine print on Diet Coke cans, Phenylalanine helps to produce the neurotransmitters norepinephrine and dopamine, as well as melanin, which gives color to the skin, hair, and eyes.

It is one of the 9 essential amino acids, so it must be received in food. It can be found in meat, milk products, and soybeans.

Too much Leucine can be unhealthy, especially for those with Phenylketonuria, (as mentioned on Diet Coke cans).

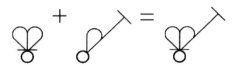

Either of these 2 mRNA codons will invoke Phenylalanine:

Uracil-Uracil-Uracil (bottom-bottom-bottom), or Uracil-Uracil-Cytosine (bottom-bottom-right).

Cysteine

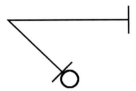

Cysteine is required for the production of nails, skin, and hair. It is also an important source for Sulfide in metabolism. When Sulfide is extracted, Cysteine becomes Alanine.

Cysteine is called conditionally-essential since in certain rare cases it cannot be produced internally by infants, the elderly, and individuals with certain metabolic diseases. Otherwise, it can be produced within the body, but it is still a good idea to receive some through food.

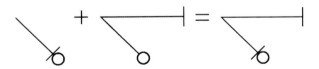

Either of these 2 mRNA codons will invoke Cysteine:

Uracil-Guanine-Uracil (bottom-left-bottom), or Uracil-Guanine-Cytosine (bottom-left-right).

Tryptophan

Tryptophan is necessary for growth, the maintenance of muscles, neurotransmitters, and many other things.

It is probably the most popular amino acid among psychonauts, as when a Carbon Dioxide molecule is removed from this Letter it becomes Tryptamine, the root of many interesting chemical compounds.

Tryptophan is one of the 9 essential amino acids, so it must be received in our food. It can be found in white meat, milk products, egg whites, as well as sunflower seeds, peanuts, pumpkin seeds, sesame seeds, and soy.

A popular pseudoscientific falsehood is the idea that the meat of turkeys contains a lot of Tryptophan, which makes Americans feel sleepy after Thanksgiving dinner. This is false, as turkeys neither contain more Tryptophan than many other foods, nor does Tryptophan make a person feel sleepy. More likely, they become drowsy after Thanksgiving dinner due to overeating, causing more of the body's resources to be directed toward digestion, with fewer resources available to keep the brain awake.

Only 1 mRNA codon can invoke Tryptophan: Uracil-Guanine-Guanine (bottom-left-left).

Glutamic Acid (Glutamate)

Popularized by Chinese restaurants, Glutamate is required to keep your brain functioning properly. Strictly speaking, when it is a Letter (amino acid) it is called Glutamic Acid. However, when it isn't spelling Words, it sheds a Hydrogen ion and becomes Glutamate, which plays a major role in learning and memory.

It is non-essential, meaning it is produced within the Human body, but it is still a good idea to receive some through food.

Either of these 2 mRNA codons will invoke Glutamic Acid:

Guanine-Adenine-Adenine (left-top-top), or Guanine-Adenine-Guanine (left-top-left).

Aspartic Acid (Aspartate)

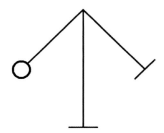

Aspartic Acid helps every cell in the body work. It helps with hormone production and release, as well as with the nervous system.

Aspartate is the salt form of Aspartic Acid (I can hear the alchemists out there getting excited). In Humans, Aspartate can be produced from Oxaloacetate, and Aspartic Acid from Aspartate. It is therefore non-essential, but it is still a good idea to receive some through food.

Plants and many micro-organisms can produce Methionine, Threonine, Isoleucine, and Lysine from Aspartate. However, Humans cannot, which is why those four are essential amino acids.

Either of these 2 mRNA codons will invoke Aspartic Acid:

Guanine-Adenine-Uracil (left-top-bottom), or Guanine-Adenine-Cytosine (left-top-right).

Valine

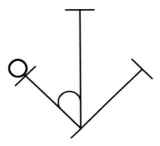

Valine can serve as an energy fuel, but only when accompanied with thiamin, riboflavin, niacin, vitamin B6, vitamin B12, pantothenate, biotin, lipoate, ubiquinone, magnesium, and iron.

It is popular for people to take Valine supplements for muscle growth, to increase athletic performance, and to boost the immune system, however it has not been proven to help with any of these.

Valine is one of the 9 essential amino acids, so it must be received in our food. It can be found in meat, fish, milk products, as well as soy, some nuts, vegetables, and whole grains.

Any of these 4 mRNA codons will invoke Valine:

Guanine-Uracil-Adenine (left-bottom-top), Guanine-Uracil-Uracil (left-bottom-bottom), Guanine-Uracil-Guanine (left-bottom-left), or Guanine-Uracil-Cytosine (left-bottom-right).

Glycine

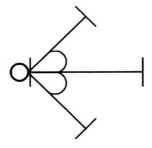

Glycine acts as neurotransmitter in the central nervous system, as well as an antioxidant, and anti-inflammatory.

It is usually considered nonessential, as it can be produced within the Human body. However, recent studies suggest that it should be considered conditionally-essential during late stages of pregnancy. Too much Glycine can be unhealthy.

Any of these 4 mRNA codons will invoke Glycine:

Guanine-Guanine-Adenine (left-left-top), Guanine-Guanine-Uracil (left-left-bottom), Guanine-Guanine-Guanine (left-left-left), or Guanine-Guanine-Cytosine (left-left-right).

Alanine

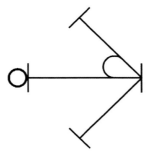

Alanine provides energy for muscles and the central nervous system. It also strengthens the immune system and helps the body to use sugars.

It is non-essential, meaning it is produced within the Human body. It can be created from the Letters Valine, Leucine, and Isoleucine. It is still a good idea to receive some through food, though.

Any of these 4 mRNA codons will invoke Alanine:

Guanine-Cytosine-Adenine (left-right-top), Guanine-Cytosine-Uracil (left-right-bottom), Guanine-Cytosine-Guanine (left-right-left), or Guanine-Cytosine-Cytosine (left-right-right).

Glutamine

Glutamine is the most abundant amino acid in the Human body. It maintains muscle protein, and helps to make other amino acids and Glucose.

It is called conditionally-essential because while it can be produced inside the body, when tissue is being built or repaired, when healing from wounds or a severe illness, it becomes necessary to receive extra Glutamine from food.

It can be found in meat, milk products, as well as beans, beets, cabbage, spinach, carrots, parsley, vegetable juices, wheat, papaya, brussels sprouts, celery, and kale. Too much Glutamine, though, can be unhealthy.

Either of these 2 mRNA codons will invoke Glutamine:

Cytosine-Adenine-Adenine (right-top-top), or Cytosine-Adenine-Guanine (right-top-left)

Histidine

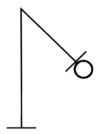

Popularized by Benadryl and other "anti-histamines" …sort of… Histidine is a precursor for Histamine, which is vital for inflammation in immune responses. Histidine also serves as a precursor to several compounds with roles in skeletal muscles.

It is one of the 9 essential amino acids, so it must be received in food. It can be found in meat and fish, as well as soy, kidney beans, peas, oats, and wheat. Too much Histidine can be unhealthy.

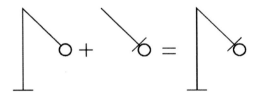

Either of these 2 mRNA codons will invoke Histidine: Cytosine-Adenine-Uracil (right-top-bottom), or Cytosine-Adenine-Cytosine (right-top-right)

Proline

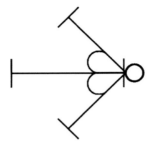

Proline helps with metabolism, nutrition, wound healing, antioxidative reactions, and immune responses. It also helps in the production of the Letter Arginine, as well as Glutamate, and other important molecules.

It is called conditionally-essential because while it can be produced inside the body, when healing from severe burns or wounds it can be necessary to receive additional Proline from food. Too much Proline can be unhealthy.

Any of these 4 mRNA codons will invoke Proline:

Cytosine-Cytosine-Adenine (right-right-top), Cytosine-Cytosine-Uracil (right-right-bottom), Cytosine-Cytosine-Guanine (right-right-left), or Cytosine-Cytosine-Cytosine (right-right-right).

III. DNA-ALPHABETICAL

A few questions may have come to mind while reading this book up to now. In the next two chapters, I hope to anticipate them, and answer them.

What is DNA-Alphabetical Order?

Okay, when I first began constructing the symbols, the sigils, to represent the codons which produce the amino acids, I started by converting everything on the codon chart to its opposite.

I reasoned that the code in DNA was the opposite of the code in the mRNA. The code in the mRNA is the one that is used to show which codons result in which amino acids. So, to link the amino acids directly to the DNA, I changed every nucleic acid to its opposite, or to that nucleic acid to which it had bonded in the DNA to receive the information.

This was a choice, back in 1996, and I'm not sure I agree with it entirely as I write this in 2022. I'll explain.

The DNA is a double-helix made up of nucleic acids which bond with one another. Thymine bonds with Adenine, and Cytosine bonds with Guanine. mRNA is a single-helix copied from a portion of the DNA.

The older folk reading this might remember, and the younger might have seen it in old movies: There was a time when a person doing a research paper might go to their local library. Of all the thousands of books and millions of pages, they might find 4 pages which they want to take with them. So, they'd take the book, or books, to the room in the library with the Xerox machines, and make photocopies.

One of the four nucleic acids of the DNA never leaves the Nucleus: Thymine. In the DNA, Thymine is always bonded with Adenine. When the mRNA copy is made, Uracil is used instead of Thymine to bond with Adenine.

So, there are five nucleic acids, and one of them never leaves the DNA, Thymine, and one of them is never present in the DNA, Uracil, but takes its place when exiting the Nucleus, like a student exiting the library to go home and write their research paper.

The mRNA, in this analogy, is the photocopy. It is made of the nucleic acids which bonded with one of the two strands of DNA, a sort of reverse-image of the one called the "anticoding strand." In the end, the mRNA leaves with a copy of the strand it didn't touch, which is called the "coding strand."

Anyway, moving forward with the explanation about DNA-Alphabetical order, the first thing you'll need to know is that I was working with the reverse of the codons traditionally associated with the amino acids.

Tetragrammaton and Pentagrammaton

To explain my thought process, it now becomes necessary to move from the pure reason and modern science side of Isaac Newton to the side of occult tradition and spiritual alchemy.

The basic idea of Tetragrammaton is that there are 4 letters in the name of God, יהוה or Yod Heh Vav Heh. (Note that Hebrew is written from right to left.) Each of these letters corresponds with a "Primal Element," י Yod with Fire, ה Heh with Water, ו Vav with Air, and ה Heh-final with Earth.

The idea of Pentagrammaton is that there are 5 letters in the name of God, והשיה or Yod Heh Shin Vav Heh, pronounced Yeheshua, and commonly known as "Jesus." The Yod, Heh, Vav, and Heh-final correspond to the same four Primal Elements, but what has been added to it is the ש Shin, which refers to a fifth Element, that of Spirit.

In the teachings of the Christianized Kabbalah, it is said that in the case of Tetragrammaton, the Spirit Element resides "above" the other four, sort of out-of-reach.

With these teachings in mind, I observed that of the five nucleic acids, Thymine is the one which is present in the Nucleus of every cell, in the DNA itself, and never exits the nucleus with the mRNA. So, it seemed very natural to assign the Spirit element to Thymine.

Adenine is the nucleic acid which bonds with Thymine, so it stood to reason that Water could be assigned to Adenine, as it is said that in the beginning the Spirit of Elohim moved upon the face of the Waters of Creation, and Yeheshua told Nicodemus, "You must be born of Water and of Spirit."

Uracil, I reasoned, would be attributed to the element of Fire. Outside the nucleus, Uracil stands in for Thymine. Something about tongues of fire descending upon the heads of the disciples at Pentecost resembling Hebrew Yods and representing Holy Spirit and Fire from Heaven, coupled with the white dove resembling Shin descending upon the head of Yeheshua when he met the Baptist, made it seem intuitive that Uracil, when standing in for Thymine, should be attributed to Fire, and that Fire and Water also bonded as opposites, Fire being active and Water being passive, the Divine Father, י Yod, bonding with the Divine Mother, ה Heh.

Examining the remaining two nucleic acids I noticed that Cytosine is a pyrimidine like Thymine and Uracil, while Guanine is a purine like Adenine. It followed, then, that Cytosine should be attributed to the active element Air and ו Vav, and Guanine to passive Earth and ה Heh-final. These correspondences were later reinforced when I saw how the molecular structures of purines differed from pyrimidines:

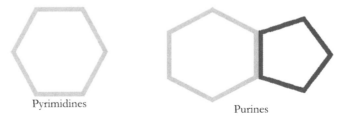

Pyrimidines

Purines

The central structure of the pyrimidines is hexagonal, and 6 is a number associated with the Sun, and the Macrocosm. The purines were a hexagon and a pentagon together, sharing one side, reminiscent of the Alchemical Marriage of Sol and Luna, Sun and Moon, Macrocosm and Microcosm.

So, given that I was working with the "anticoding" strand's reversed codons, and that I had assigned Thymine basically to י Yod, Adenine to ה Heh, Cytosine to ו Vav, and Guanine to ה Heh-final, and there is a pre-existing pecking-order within the name יהוה Yod Heh Vav Heh itself, it may now become clear what DNA-Alphabetical Order is:

The Letter produced by the codon Thymine-Thymine-Thymine should come first, followed by Thymine-Thymine-Adenine. Eventually, at the very end, will come Guanine-Guanine-Guanine.

That said, since modern science uses the codons of either the "coding" strand of the DNA or those of the mRNA, this means that, when looking at the mRNA, the codon Adenine-Adenine-Adenine comes first, followed by Adenine-Adenine-Uracil, and the very last Letter would be that of the codon Cytosine-Cytosine-Cytosine.

IV. THE KEY

Now that that's all as clear as mud, we can move on to how all of this translates into the particular shapes of the letters. Specifically…

Why are the nucleic acids assigned to those four points in particular?

In traditional, perhaps subtly problematic, western esotericism, the active (masculine) י Yod, is before or above the passive (feminine) ה Heh. In the Major Arcana of a common Tarot deck, י Yod, in this context, is associated with the Kings and Fire, and ה Heh with the Queens and Water. This is reflected as well in regular playing cards.

However, rather than only Jacks remaining, there are two more Court Cards, usually called Knights and Pages. Sometimes, in more esoteric decks, these two are called Princes and Princesses. The Princes refer to ו Vav and Air, and the Princesses to ה Heh-final and Earth.

With these things in mind, I assigned Thymine (Fire, or Spirit) to the upper-most point, and Adenine (Water), with which it bonds, to the bottom point. Then, I assigned Cytosine (Air) to the point on the left, and Guanine (Earth) to the point on the right.

This might seem counter-intuitive, since the right hand is usually considered the more dominant and active, and the left hand more passive. Perhaps I was being progressive assigning the masculine element to the left and the feminine to the right? Well, not really...

See, when a person is initiated in a Golden Dawn style temple, as they stand in the west facing east they'll see two pillars. The one on the left is The Black Pillar associated with גבורה Geburah and Power, the one on the right is The White Pillar associated with חסד Chesed and Mercy. When you look at a diagram of The Tree of Life, it is the same, גבורה Geburah and The Black Pillar are on the left side, חסד Chesed and The White Pillar are on the right:

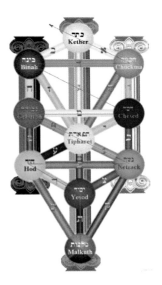

However, when The Tree of Life to which these pillars refer is placed on the Human body, The Black Pillar is on the right side of the body, and The White Pillar is on the left side.

The reason for this is simple: When you look at the diagram of The Tree of Life it is as if you are looking at a person facing you. So, right and left are reversed. In the temple, when you stand between the two pillars and become, as it were, the image of The Tree of Life itself, you stand facing west rather than east. If you stand to the east of the pillars facing west, or if you stand between the pillars facing west, The Black Pillar is on your own right side, and The White Pillar is on your left.

Similarly, Cytosine, attributed to active Air, being assigned to the point on the left means it is on its own right side. Guanine, attributed to passive Earth, being on the right means that it is on its own left.

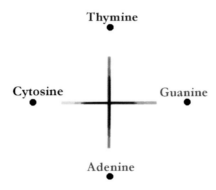

I remember showing all of this to a student of these mysteries who responded, "You lost me with the placement of the elements in the four directions, this isn't like the LBRP, the BRH, the Kerubs, it's not even like the Rose Cross Lamen, where did you get this from?" Well, just because I'm part troll, I'd like to offer another perspective:

The 5 Dhyani Buddhas

Although, in the case of the 5 Dhyani Buddhas, the top of the diagram refers to the west, and yellow is associated with Earth and green is associated with Air, so perhaps that's not as helpful as it appears at first glance, for our purposes here, though it may help with memorization.

All of that being said, since it was to the codons of the "anticoding" strand of the DNA that I was assigning these positions, when looking at the mRNA or the "coding" strand, which is the one used by all of modern science, the amino acids become those of the mRNA which bond to these. Thus, Thymine becomes Adenine, Adenine becomes Uracil, Guanine becomes Cytosine, and Cytosine becomes Guanine, thus:

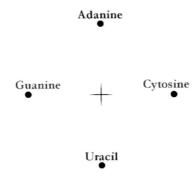

V. THE WORDS

If amino acids are the Letters, then peptides and proteins are the Words. Put simply, short words are called peptides, longer words are called proteins.

Spoken and written words of Human language act as metaphors for things, actions, ideas and so on, for the sake of communication. DNA Words, on the other hand, tend to be more like small creatures. They are born, they work and play in various ways depending on their heredities and environments, and they eventually pass away. They are quite diverse, and the tasks they perform in the grand tapestry of Organic Life is mind-boggling, complex, and often beautiful.

What is presented in this book is very simplified for the purpose of showing a glimpse of the whole picture. From space, you can see the whole world at once, or at least the half that's facing you, but the individual mountains, people, insects and such are difficult to make out. After reading this book, if you find yourself wanting to know more, the good news is there is plenty more to learn.

In the DNA, every Word begins with ＼ and ends with ◁. They are like the spaces and punctuation of the DNA. When Words are copied directly from the DNA, it can be assumed that these START and STOP commands come before the first Letter and after the last.

Sometimes Words are produced indirectly, rather than being written directly in the DNA. A person might read about the Kerubim of Ezekiel and exclaim, "Far out!" However, the words "Far out" are not written in the book of Ezekiel. Similarly, two or three Words may be written in the DNA, copied to the mRNA, which are then read and constructed by the ribosomes, resulting in enzymes which specialize in working together to construct a simple peptide, or small Word.

The example Words in this chapter were chosen because they are short. Most Words have hundreds or even thousands of Letters. A couple examples of these longer ones are in the next chapter, "Endogenous."

The longer Words are more often written directly in the DNA, where the shorter Words (peptides) are often created by longer Words (enzymes) sometimes by using parts of even longer Words (proteins). This is one way that The Natural Language differs from, say, English.

The Words which come directly from the DNA and mRNA always use the 20 Letters of The DNA Alphabet presented in this book, but those produced indirectly by other Words will often have other variations of these Letters, amino acids which aren't among those written in the DNA. I liken these to Letters that have áccent marks, where the DNA itself only uses Letters without accent marks.

Here are a few examples of the approximately 20,000 different Words conversing inside the Human body. They are given, of course, in DNA-Alphabetical order.

Substance P

Substance P is a Word of 11 Letters. It is a neuropeptide which can act as both a neurotransmitter and a neuromodulator. It is found in the brain in regions specific to regulating emotion, as well as the linings of capillaries, lymphatics, stem cells, white blood cells, and many tissues and organs. It is associated with mood regulation, anxiety, stress, reinforcement, respiratory rhythm, neurotoxicity, and pain. It also has anti-microbial properties.

Substance P is not directly written in the DNA, but is derived from a Word of 129 Letters, Preprotachykinin-1, whose name is written in the number 7 chromosome of the Human DNA.

•

Bradykinin

Bradykinin is a Word of 9 Letters. It is a peptide which causes arterioles to enlarge, promotes inflammation, and decreases blood pressure. It plays a role in fetal development, and is also involved in the mechanism of pain.

It is written in the number 14 chromosome of the Human DNA.

•

Oxytocin

Oxytocin is a Word of 9 Letters. It is one of the most well-known neuropeptides, and is sometimes called "The Love Hormone" due to its connection with sexual intercourse and social bonding. It also has a prominent role in child-birth and breast-feeding.

Oxytocin is not directly constructed by ribosomes reading mRNA copies of DNA. Rather, several enzymes written in the DNA work together to produce Oxytocin.

Strictly speaking, the last of its amino acids is Glycineamide, a precursor to Glycine, so the above Word is not entirely accurate (like writing "Jerome" instead of "Jérôme").

•

Angiotensin II

Angiotensin II is a Word of 8 Letters, a peptide which contracts arterial muscles, resulting in blood vessels narrowing, decreasing blood flow and raising blood pressure.

The last of Angiotensin II's amino acids is Phenylalamine, which is derived from Phenylalanine. So, the DNA Alphabet spelling of the Word is not entirely accurate (like writing "Jalapeno" instead of "Jalapeño").

Angiotensin II is produced from a Word of 10 Letters, Angiotensin I. Angiotensin I is converted to Angiotensin II by a Word of 615 Letters, an enzyme called ACE.

Angiotensin I comes from a Word of 485 Letters, Angiotensinogen, whose name is written in the number 17 chromosome of the Human DNA.

•

Somatostatin

Somatostatin is a Word of 14 Letters, also called "Growth-Hormone-Inhibiting-Hormone." It has strong regulatory effects throughout the body.

It, along with a Word of 28 Letters which is also called Somatostatin, are both derived from Prepro-Somatostatin whose name is written in the number 3 chromosome of the Human DNA.

•

Alpha-MSH

Alpha-Melanocyte Stimulating Hormone is a Word of 13 Letters. It stimulates skin pigmentation, helps regulate inflammation, and has antimicrobial properties.

It is derived from a Word of 39 Letters, Adrenocorticotropic Hormone, which itself is derived from a Word of 241 Letters, Pro-opiomelanocortin, whose name is written in the number 2 chromosome of the Human DNA.

VI. ENDOGENOUS

Without incriminating myself too much, I'll just say that in late 2011 I became very interested in Dimethyltryptamine. I noticed that the effect it had on the brain was similar to experiences I'd had at certain points throughout my life. In particular, it reminded me of the effect of certain Tibetan Tantric Yoga practices which my dad had taught me when I was very young.

I wanted to learn more about how it was produced in the Human brain. I remembered, and dug through my old papers and notebooks until I found my old Practicus journal, the notebook in which I'd written all of my thoughts back in 1996, and there it was: The DNA Alphabet I'd come up with that day in Biology class.

I did a bit of digging online, with the goal of writing the names of the 2 enzymes responsible for the production of Dimethyltryptamine in the Human brain. The names of these two enzymes are written in the DNA, in the number 7 chromosome of every cell of every Human being in the world.

"Tryptophan Decarboxalayse" is also known by other names, and has other functions as well. Its name, in The Natural Language, has 480 Letters. One of its jobs, abilities, or pastimes if you will, is to find a lone Tryptophan...

...and to remove from it a Carbon-Dioxide, which is then carried by the blood to the lungs, and exhaled eventually. What's left, after Carbon-Dioxide has been removed from a Tryptophan, is called Tryptamine.

Then along comes another enzyme called "Indolethylamine N-Methyltransferase," whose name has 262 Letters. It takes the Tryptamine molecule, and methylates it twice. In other words, it adds a Carbon atom with 3 Hydrogen atoms. It does this twice, in key places.

Now, Dimethyltryptamine doesn't last long in the Human body before a certain communist-dictator enzyme called MAO comes along and takes it apart. (it's not really a communist-dictator, I'm just making a pun.) The Shamans of Peru know about this one, though they may not call it by these scientific names. It's a kindness, really, since if one has too much Dimethyltryptamine in the brain, one cannot effectively defend themselves against hungry tigers, oncoming busses, or things like that.

Anyhow, for those who might be interested in knowing the names of these two enzymes in The Natural Language, using The DNA Alphabet, I've provided them here, complete with the proper DNA-grammar of starting with START and ending with STOP:

Tryptophan Decarboxalayse

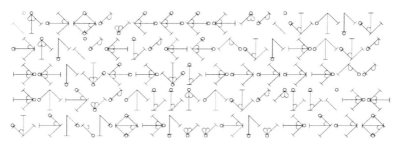

42

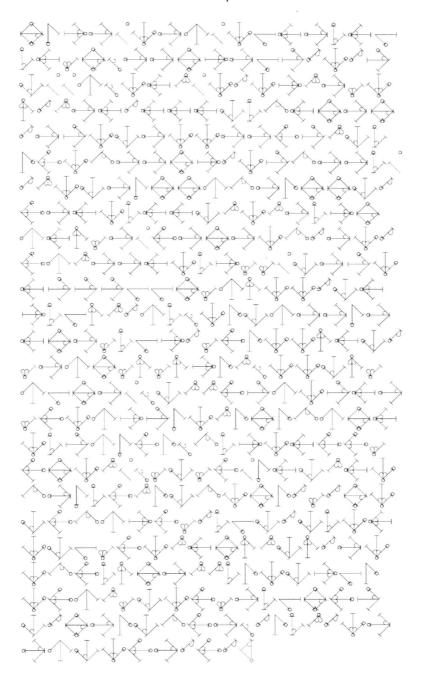

Indolethylamine N-Methyltransferase

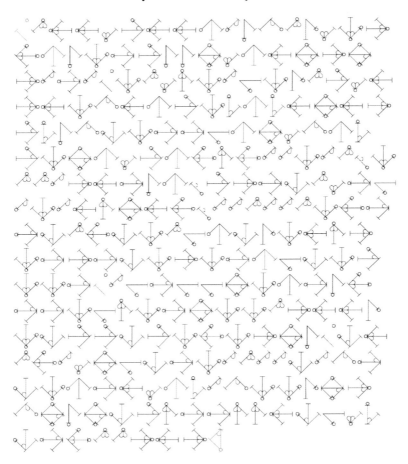

VII. CONCLUSION

So, where do I start?

Of course, this is not a question which everyone who reads this will be asking. Some will finish the book, set it aside, and think, "That was weird." Others, "Interesting." For those of you who might be asking, "So, where do I start?" here is my suggestion:

If you're new to a lot of these concepts, a good place to start is YouTube, searching for "Crash Course DNA." Hank Green's Crash Course series is so universally loved these days that college courses often require watching it as homework.

Then, you might begin by sitting in a quiet room. With your hand, trace the + symbol in front of you, starting with the vertical line from top to bottom, then the horizontal line from left to right.

When your hand begins at the top, say quietly, "Adenine." When it reaches the bottom, say, "Uracil." When it begins on the left side, say, "Guanine." When it reaches the right side, say, "Cytosine." Do this slowly, until you have it memorized.

Then, you might begin with Lysine. Note that when drawing in this way the small circle and the perpendicular line are not necessary to trace in the air, but rather indicate where to start and where to end. Trace the first codon, then the second, and visualize the complete letter before you. Repeat this slowly until you have it memorized. Then do the same for the other 19 letters, plus the STOP command.

Once all of this has been absorbed, you might try invoking a peptide. Research the peptide, and determine what music, incense, or other accompaniment might help you to key in to its energy. If calling upon Oxytocin, you might hold your favorite stuffed animal, or pet a small cat, while you are invoking it. The various codons of each Letter can all be drawn over the same + before you, or you might write them out on a piece of paper as they're written in The Words section of this book.

You can also do further research. Read about the peptides, learn about the enzymes. Find the amino acid sequences. One good resource is GenomeNet.

I really believe that the more people learn The DNA Alphabet, and The Language of Life, the more harmonious we will be as individuals and as a collective. It is very important to listen to Medical Professionals, but if we leave this knowledge solely in the hands of specialists, who are often motivated by profit, the Human Race will surely reap what it sews. Further, this knowledge is about more than survival, but quality of life. The orchestra will play until the grand finale, but we have the power not just to prolong the song, but to compose and conduct the music as well.

Mind and body are already connected, but many of us ignore the body and allow the mind to drift off. Some philosophies overtly or covertly despise the body. But even if you look at it as a mere temporary vehicle, if you have to drive your car to work every day, it's worth it to pay attention to when it needs an oil change or a wash.

Further, if you are one of those who believes that Angels can understand you when you're speaking Enochian or Hebrew, it shouldn't be too much of a leap of faith to believe that your own DNA, which you already direct with your thoughts, can understand you when you're speaking its own language.

ABOUT THE AUTHOR

Edward was born in 1978, began practicing Tibetan Tantric Yoga in 1984, and in 1993 began Wicca training with the Druidic Craft of the Wise of America, graduating from the advanced course in 1995.

In November of 1994, he was given the name Frater BT at his Golden Dawn style Neophyte initiation. In 1997, he was upgraded to H Frater BT and began teaching, and in January of 2000 he became known as VH Frater BT.

In 2013 he left the Order, in 2015 he became a Certified Yoga Instructor, and in 2017 he left California permanently and eventually settled in India where he now lives with his wife, Priyal.

He has been working, gradually, on an autobiographical fiction called "The Esoterinerd," though it may be a while yet before it is finished.

In the meantime, he hopes that you enjoyed this book, and invites you to listen to, or watch, him and many interesting guests discuss a wide variety of esoteric subjects on **VH Frater BT's Esoterinerd Podcast**, by pointing your camera phone here:

Made in the USA
Middletown, DE
18 October 2022

12992975R00031